Selling Your Price

*How to escape the race to
the bargain basement.*

DUANE SPARKS

The Sales Board, Inc.

Copyright © 2005 by Duane Sparks

Selling Your Price is available at special discounts when purchased in bulk for premiums and sales promotions as well as for fund-raising or educational use. Special editions or book excerpts can also be created to specification. For details, contact The Sales Board at the address below.

The Sales Board, Inc.

15200 25th Ave. N.
Minneapolis, MN 55447
(800) 232-3485
www.TheSalesBoard.com

ISBN: 0-9753569-6-8

Printed in the United States of America

First Printing January 2005

FORWARD

I like a lot of things about this book, but if I had to pick a favorite it would be the way the character Christine thinks and talks about "commodities." She says there is no such thing as a salesperson who is stuck selling raw, undifferentiated commodities that customers could buy from any number of suppliers, the sole significant difference being price. There are only salespeople who *think* that's what they're stuck doing.

CHS, where I work, is a diversified Fortune 500 company providing essential grain, food and energy resources with over $10 billion annual sales. Our energy products are marketed under the Cenex® brand, including a fast growing network of over 800 Cenex branded convenience stores. I hate it when I hear any of our products — like propane gas — referred to as commodities. Sure, our customers can buy propane from hundreds of suppliers; it all comes out of the same pipe. But they can only get Cenex propane from us. Our best salespeople are the ones who know how to make that meaningful. And since it is not our business strategy to be the low-cost supplier, they need to create meaning and value around something other than price.

Every job at CHS, and every family of every CHS employee, depends on the success of our salespeople. We have three types of sales reps. The first group I think of as soldiers — steady, hard-working, but not outstanding. Next are the gladiators—ultra-competitive types who win most of the sales contests.

Since we introduced the *Action Selling* system at CHS, however, a third type has emerged. I call them the orchestrators. They excel at orchestrating the sales process. They don't sell propane, they sell a warm house on a cold day. But it's more than that. They sell in a way that builds a higher level of trust and a richer relationship with customers. They win their price against cheaper suppliers because customers see real value in those relationships.

The orchestrators are the ones who ensure the future of our company. They're the ones who have mastered *Action Selling*.

I was already a believer in the *Action Selling* system before I read this book. If you weren't, I suspect you soon will be. Price competition is every bit as dangerous and destructive as Duane Sparks paints it, both to companies and to the future of the sales profession. And the solution this story describes with such clarity and power really is the only sustainable way for salespeople to escape the race to the bargain basement. Because no matter what products or services you sell, your competitors probably sell something out of the same pipe.

Do yourself a favor and start turning pages.

David L. Winkler
CES and Training Coordinator
CHS

Introduction

The case of the incredible vanishing margin.

L et me guess.

Your competitors are killing you on price. Your margins are shrinking to the vanishing point as customers challenge you to meet or beat the lowest price available for the goods or services you sell. Your company's profits are taking a hit. If margin-based commissions play a role in your compensation, your own wallet is taking a hit. And that's true even if your sales volume is up, you're gaining more clients, and you're working harder.

Your company has tried to differentiate its goods or services with guarantees, "partnership" programs, and other value-add strategies to let you compete on some basis other than price. But so have your competitors. Their value-add strategies look almost as much like yours as their products do. Like almost all goods and services, these strategies, too, have become commodities. Even if you come up with a tactic that is genuinely new and different, competitors can quickly copy it. And your customers go right back to hammering you on price.

Month after month, year after year, the price pressure increases.

You feel trapped in a race to the bargain basement, with no way out. That's depressing enough to begin with. But it gets worse. Since ultimately there can be only one price leader in any industry, you're going to lose the race — unless your entire business strategy is built upon being the lowest-cost provider. Which it isn't. Meanwhile, your margins continue to shrink.

How am I doing? Did I guess right? If so, you're going to be awfully glad you bought this book. It offers hope. It shows you an exit door that can let you escape the race to the bargain basement. And if you're in sales, you need to escape, believe me, because here's a thought that is even more chilling:

If the customer's buying decision is only about price, *what do companies need salespeople for?* There are a lot of cheaper ways to present customers with a low-price offer, or to match the competition's prices, than to pay a sales force to do it. If salespeople cannot add some value to the equation that justifies a higher price in the customer's mind, then salespeople are just additional overhead. If it's all about price, salespeople are dinosaurs, doomed to extinction by the Internet, direct mail, radio, television, and other forms of advertising and communication.

That's the bad news. The good news is, you're holding an insurance policy right now.

Maybe you've never heard of the sales system called Action Selling. In that case, this whole book will be a revelation. Or maybe you read my previous book, *Action Selling: How to Sell Like a Professional, Even If You Think You are One*. Maybe — like the character Scott in the story you're about to read — you have even taken an Action Selling training program.

Regardless, I'm pretty sure that, like Scott, you don't fully appreciate the implications of Action Selling as an escape hatch — a way out of the race to the bargain basement. I don't think I fully appreciated them myself until I started writing this book. And I'm the guy who created the Action Selling system.

You're not alone

How was I able to guess your situation accurately? To begin with, I just had to look at the world we all live in today. Customers are bombarded constantly by advertising promising lower prices. The Internet has altered shopping habits; it's quicker and easier than ever for customers to discover, compare, and buy competitive products — usually based on price. Products and services across all industries have been commodified to the point where their features and benefits are hard to distinguish. That leaves price as the sole decision point. Unless...

Unless salespeople can give buyers a compelling reason to focus on something else — a value proposition that earns and justifies a higher price in the customer's mind. And it has to be a form of value that can't easily be copied or cloned by competitors.

There is another reason I'm able to guess that you're fighting a losing battle with the margin demon. It's because you have so much company. In 2004 The Sales Board conducted a national survey focusing on price competition. The survey targeted C-level executives, vice presidents and sales directors, and sales professionals. Here are a few key findings that illustrate the problem, some of its complicating factors — and the reasons for hope.

The Sales Board National Price Competition Study

Where is the Pain?

Sales up, but margins shrinking: 80% of respondents report that sales volume is increasing. But more than half (51%) say their margins are eroding. Even among those with growing sales, 40% are increasing volume at the expense of margins.

The price wars are getting worse: 89% say that price competition is a growing issue.

My wallet is shrinking! Three out of five say their personal income is being impacted by price competition.

What Sales Managers Know Is Broken But Can't Fix

Failure to differentiate is the No. 1 problem: Sales directors and VPs identified the inability to find a differentiated sales position as the leading reason why their salespeople resort to discounting to match competitors' prices.

Most companies are trying to differentiate: 56 percent say their companies use "partnering" or other value-add strategies to try to differentiate themselves.

Fewer than one in five salespeople deal effectively with price objections: Only 19% of sales directors and sales professionals rate themselves as "effective" at handling a price objection. (C-level respondents think their sales forces are far better than that.)

What the C-Level Doesn't Know

They think they're competing on value: Fewer than 1% of C-level execs said their business strategy is to be the industry price leader. That means 99% are trying to compete, somehow, on the basis of value.

But discounting rules: More than half of all salespeople say they give discounts to match competitors' prices at least 70% of the time. Either the value-strategy message isn't getting through, the tactics don't work, or salespeople aren't equipped to carry them out.

Salespeople unaware of competition's strategies: When asked about partnering strategies and other tactics their major competitors use to justify higher prices, 43% of sales professionals answered "I don't know."

No Sales Process Exists. The C-level thinks salespeople are following a consistent selling procedure 50% more often than sales management actually observes.

But There is Hope

Some salespeople DO drive higher margins: 86% of all respondents agree that top-performing salespeople generate higher margins. (So there must be ways out of the price trap!)

Quality sales relationships win business: Respondents in every category agreed that when customers do buy from them instead of their competitors, the No. 1 reason is because of a relationship with a salesperson—not product features, not company reputation, and not price.

The Sales Board's National Price Competition Study was conducted via the Internet in August-September 2004. Of the 722 respondents in numerous industries, 23% were C-level executives, 36% were vice presidents or sales directors, and 41% were active sales professionals. For a white paper with details and complete results of the study, contact TheSalesBoard.com or (800) 232-3485.

Opt out of the race

It boils down to this: The opponent is price competition. The battlefield is the customer's mind. The reality is that most products and services have become undifferentiated commodities. To justify their existence and earn their keep, salespeople must add some kind of value that differentiates their offerings. They must give buyers a compelling reason to pay more for their goods and services than for very similar ones they can get cheaper.

Guarantees and other wrap-around tactics aimed at adding that perceived value don't work very well because they quickly become commodities too. So salespeople fall back on discounting and price matching as the only way to get or keep their customers' business.

And every time salespeople cave into pressure to match or beat a competitor's price, *they are teaching their own customers to focus on price and to ask for more discounts next time.* Have your competitors really forced you into the race to the bargain basement? Or are you right in there leading the pack, perpetuating the cycle?

If you're in a rigged poker game, the only way to win is to kick over the table. If you're in a doomed race, the only solution is to opt out of it. But how?

The answer doesn't lie in *what* you sell but *how* you sell. Maybe you've heard that before. But the usual recipes for attacking the dilemma with sales training are aimed at the wrong targets.

Myth: Salespeople need to get better at closing.

Reality: They need to get better at opening.

Myth: Salespeople need to become better price negotiators.

Reality: They need a way to sell that takes the focus off price negotiation altogether.

What's needed is a systematic approach to selling that reliably puts price in its correct perspective in the customer's mind—as just one part of an overall value equation. I humbly suggest (all right, not so humbly) that Action Selling is that system. To explain why, I want to tell you a story about a sales rep named Scott and his manager, Christine. They happen to be in the dental-supply business. But I think you'll find that Scott's problems sound an awful lot like yours. The solution he discovers can be yours as well.

At the risk of spoiling some suspense, I'll tell you one thing Scott learns that should give us all great cause for hope. *The price haggling/discounting game is as big a trap for many customers as it is for salespeople.* A lot of your business clients would be more than happy to stop nickeling and diming their precious time away with constant bargain hunting. They're glad to find a justifiable reason to escape the trap. You just need to give them one.

Together with Scott, you're about to crack the case of the incredible vanishing margin.

I wish you every success. Good Action Selling!

Duane Sparks
Chairman
The Sales Board, Inc.

CONTENTS

PREFACE

The race to the bargain basement.

Scott walked into Christine's office on a January Monday morning with no idea what to expect. When you're a sales rep and the branch sales manager asks if you have some time to meet with her, you make the time. So here he was.

"Hi, Scott. Grab a chair," Christine said, gesturing at six seats surrounding the small, round conference table she used for informal meetings. "How's it going?"

"Can't complain," he said. "New year, same battle."

Scott was a bit intimidated by Christine, but he respected her more than any manager he'd known. She was all business, but she certainly knew her stuff. When she joined the company a year ago, she had persuaded the powers-that-be at corporate headquarters to introduce a new sales system called Action Selling. As far as Scott was concerned, Action Selling was the best thing that ever happened to his career. And he wasn't alone. Sales reps around the country regarded the new system as a gift from heaven. Christine was a rising star at Partner Dental Supply, expected to move up in the company and fast.

Characteristically, Christine wasted no time but got straight to the point. "I've been going over your numbers," she said, indicating a printout on the table in front of her. "You increased your volume by 10 percent last year. And it looks like you picked up, what, seven net new customers?"

"Eight," Scott said proudly.

"That's great," Christine said. "Congratulations. But here's what I'm wondering: In the prior year, you had almost exactly $1 million in sales. Last year you boosted it to $1.1 million. There's your 10 percent rise in volume."

Scott smiled.

"But while your volume went up," Christine continued, "your margins slipped by 3.5 percent. In the prior year your average gross margin was 35 percent, right in line with our branch norms. Last year your territory dropped to 31.5 percent."

"Our competitors are killing me on price. All of them."

Scott stopped smiling. *Like I didn't know that?* he thought. "Tell me about it," he groaned. "Our competitors are killing me on price. All of them."

"But company-wide, margins actually increased by 1 percent last year," Christine said.

"They did?" Scott was genuinely astonished.

"I just received the year-end numbers," she said. "Nationally, margins are up 1 percent. But margins for the Los Angeles branch rose only 0.8 percent. That puts us slightly behind the company average. And your territory accounts for most of the shortfall."

Scott shifted nervously in his chair. "Well, I don't know what's going on with our other sales reps, but it can't be what's happening to me," he said. "All of my clients are

> *"I have to match competitor's prices or lose my customer's business."*

cutting costs. Every day I have to fight like a dog to save my accounts from cut-rate offers from competitors trying to get in the door. I have to match their prices or lose my customers' business."

"Do you?" Christine asked. The question hung in the air. *I'll just tell that to the Western regional manager when he calls me on the carpet to explain why my branch can't keep up,* she thought. *"Well, Gary, I've got a rep named Scott who has no choice but to discount whenever he runs into price competition. Nothing to be done about it, you know." Yeah, that'll get me where I want to go in this company.*

Scott didn't like the look on Christine's face. For a long moment, she appeared to be wondering whether to terminate him. Then she collected herself and grabbed a notepad.

"First let's make sure we understand what's happening," Christine said. "In the prior year, you did a gross margin of 35 percent. In the year that just ended, you did $1.1 million in sales at a gross margin of 31.5 percent. That's a drop of 3.5 percent. Factor in the 1 percent company increase, and you're short 4.5 percent," she said, her pen scratching the pad. "So despite the fact that your volume increased to $1.1 million, Partner Dental made $49,500 less money on your sales. And since your commission is based on gross profit, you made less too — even though you had more clients and more work to do."

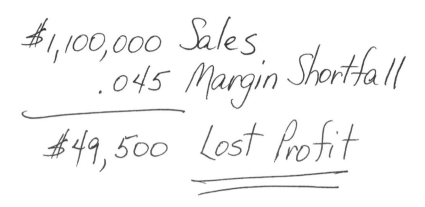

$1,100,000 Sales
.045 Margin Shortfall
―――――――――
$49,500 Lost Profit

"Yeah, I noticed that," Scott said, careful to keep the sarcasm muted. *So did my wife,* he thought, remembering an unpleasant Saturday when he had tried to explain how it came to pass that he was working longer hours and picking up new clients but actually making less money.

> *He was working longer hours and adding clients, but making less money.*

"So we agree that maintaining margin is important both for the company and for you personally?" Christine asked.

"Of course," Scott answered.

"But you have no option except to cut your prices to match the competition's lowest offer?" she asked.

"Hey, you don't know what it's like out there!" Scott protested. Even as he spoke, however, he knew this wasn't true. Christine had an excellent grasp of what was going on in the field.

But she didn't argue with him. "Maybe I don't," she said agreeably. "Can you give me an example?"

"I can give you a hundred examples," Scott said. "Just last week I called on Dr. Wright at his dental office in Santa Monica. I'm barely in the door when Susan, his office manager, shows me a flyer she got from Discount Dental Supply. They're running a sale on surface disinfectant — 64-ounce bottles for $14.95. It's the same disinfectant I sell them for $15.95. Susan says their practice is feeling the economic squeeze, and Dr. Wright has told her to cut costs on consumable supplies. She asks if I can match the competitor's price.

"What can I do?" Scott concluded. "It's the same disinfectant. So I tell her, yeah, I'll match the $14.95 price. It's either that or watch her buy it from Discount Dental. This kind of thing is happening in my territory every day. I've never seen it this brutal. And it keeps getting worse. Everybody is trying to cut costs to the bone."

"I see," Christine said. "And this Discount Dental flyer was sent only to dentists who happen to be your accounts?"

"No," Scott admitted, reddening. "But the point is, the products we sell are exactly the same as the ones our customers can buy from our competitors. And when the economy is pinching their business, customer loyalty goes out the window."

"That's certainly one point," Christine agreed. "But it raises another point, doesn't it? If we want to compete on any basis except

"...unless we give them a good reason, why should they pay more?"

being the lowest-cost provider, our customers have to perceive some added value in dealing with us, right? I mean, unless we give them a good reason, why *should* they pay more to do business with us?"

"Yes, but you don't know what it's..." Scott began again, lamely.

"There's another point," Christine interrupted. "If the only thing our salespeople can do about price competition is to match the lowest price out there, why should Partner Dental add to its overhead by paying salespeople? We could play the low-cost game with nothing but direct mail and the Internet, couldn't we?"

"If the only thing our salespeople can do is to match the lowest price, why pay salespeople?"

That one jolted him. "Good salespeople develop relationships with customers that the Internet could never match," Scott protested.

"But Susan the office manager was ready to desert you for a difference of one dollar?" Christine asked quietly.

Scott said nothing. *I thought I was doing pretty well, considering,* he thought. *Is my job on the line here?*

Knowing that she had Scott's full attention, Christine switched tacks. "Aren't you finding that the new Action Selling system helps you avoid a lot of price objections?" she asked.

The question surprised him. "Action Selling is great," he said.

"How do you think I got those eight new clients? But it isn't my new clients who are hammering me on price. It's the long-term ones."

His answer seemed to surprise Christine in turn. *So you're telling me you aren't discounting to get your new business,* she thought. *I'll bet the invoices would say otherwise.* She chose not to challenge him on it, however. His margin numbers gave her all the ammunition she needed to let Scott know that something had to change. "You think of Action Selling as a system that applies only to gaining new business?" she asked.

"Oh, I know we're supposed to use it with existing customers too," he said quickly. "But there aren't as many opportunities when you're making route calls on customers you already know well. In fact, I've been wondering if I could use some training on negotiation skills to help me counter price issues like the one I had with Susan."

"I see," Christine said thoughtfully. "So you don't think that Action Selling applies as well or as often when you're talking to current customers as when you're calling on new prospects. Is that right?"

"Well, it's not that the principles don't apply," Scott said. "It's just that there isn't time to plan and orchestrate every call on existing customers the way I do with new ones. The dynamics of the calls are different. And the price pressure out there really is incredible, Christine."

"Scott, do you remember how Action Selling defines an objection — including a price objection?"

"Sure," he said. "Action Selling defines an objection as *a cus-*

"Action Selling defines an objection as a customer's response to an unasked question."

tomer's response to an unasked *question.* But when Susan is holding a flyer that offers her the same disinfectant for less money, what question did I fail to ask her?"

"Excellent!" Christine said, surprising him.

"Huh?"

"That's exactly what you should be asking yourself," Christine said. "Scott, doesn't it seem that Action Selling offers you an alternative to matching or beating competitors' prices on an item-by-item basis? Shouldn't Action Selling be something you do *instead of* negotiating price?"

"Well," Scott said, trying to regroup, "of course I know that Action Selling helps to keep the price issue in its proper perspective as just one part of a value equation. But seriously, Christine, what question can I ask customers like Susan when they're under pressure to cut costs and somebody else has a lower price on the same product I'm selling?"

"I have a hunch about that," Christine said. "It has to do with something you just said: 'value equation.' But let's see if we can figure it out together." *You can lead a horse to water but you can't make it drink,* she thought. *Am I being unfair because Action Selling is so clear to me while it's new to him? I don't know if you're going to make the grade, Scott, and if you can't, you aren't going to take me down with you. But for now, let's see if you get it.*

"Suppose we start with a quick review of the Action Selling system," Christine said. "You say it works wonderfully to win over new clients. But 90 percent of your business comes from existing clients, and Action Selling should be helping you find ways to add value that justifies higher margins with them. In fact, I say that's how most other reps in our branch have managed to increase their margins despite the same brutal price competition you're facing."

Ouch! Scott thought. *You're not playing around, are you? But if other reps are increasing their margins in this environment, then I guess I must be missing something, all right. Hope I can keep my job long enough to find out what it is.*

"Why don't you tell me how you use Action Selling when you call on new prospects," Christine continued. "Maybe along the way we'll discover if I'm right

> *"Action Selling is more than a method for keeping price in perspective — it can be an alternative to negotiating price."*

when I claim that Action Selling is more than a method for keeping price in perspective — that it actually can be an alternative to negotiating on the prices of individual items we sell."

"Hey," Scott said, "If you can show me a way out of this price-cutting nightmare, I'm game." *So is my wife*, he thought. "Well, you know how Action Selling works, of course…"

"No, I'd like you to explain it to me, please," Christine said. She leaned back in her chair looking attentive.

Okay, Scott thought. *Here goes.*

Chapter 1

HOW PROFESSIONALS SELL

Action Selling in action.

S cott opened his briefcase and fished out two things. One was an ordinary notepad. The other was a colorful laminated card. One side of the card illustrated "The Action Selling Process." The other side showed something called the "Ask the Best Questions Map." *Take note, Christine*, he thought. *I not only saved this card from the training program, I carry it with me wherever I go.*

IIe laid the card on the table and picked up the notepad. "You want me to explain this as if you don't know it?" he asked.

"Just walk me through the process quickly," Christine said.

"All right," Scott began, happy to demonstrate that he understood and appreciated the system that Christine herself had introduced to Partner Dental. "Action Selling is a step-by-step system for managing a sales call — actually, for managing the entire sales process, from the planning stage to following up after a sale. It's based on the documented fact that every customer makes five crucial buying decisions in the course of any major sale. And whether the customer realizes it or not, these decisions are always made in the same order."

On his notepad Scott drew a large question mark, divided it into sections, and labeled each section.

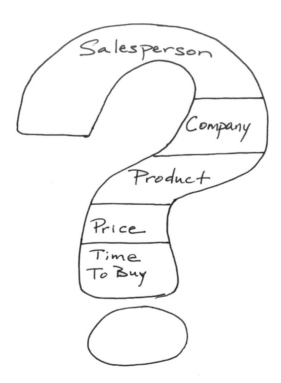

"First," he said, "the customer decides whether to 'buy' the salesperson. This means that I can't sell my product until I have first sold myself. Does the customer like me? More importantly, does he trust me? Does he believe that I understand his needs and that I want to help him instead of just taking his money?"

Scott ran briefly through the four remaining buying decisions. After customers have 'bought' the salesperson, they consider the company the salesperson represents (Is it reputable? Is it a good match for the customer's company?). Then they make a decision about the product (Is it the right solution for me? How does it compare with competitive offerings?). Then they consider the price (Is the product worth the money?). Finally, they consider the "time to buy" (How urgent is the need for the product and when must I decide?).

"The important thing to remember about the five buying decisions," Scott said, "is that customers will not seriously consider any later decisions until the previous ones have been made. A customer who wants to focus on my product or my price before I've sold myself and my company is doing both of us a disservice. Action Selling provides a

> *"...price is decision number four on the list of five."*

framework and methods for keeping a sales call on track so that it follows the customer's natural decision-making process."

"So you're telling me that price is decision number four on that list of five?" Christine asked.

"Well, yes," Scott said defensively, "but when a customer

already knows about your product and she's looking at the same thing for less money..."

"Hold that thought, please," Christine said. "Sorry I interrupted. Please go on. What is Action Selling, exactly?"

Scott took a deep breath. Then he pushed the laminated card to the center of the table between them. "Action Selling says that every sales call is like a drama with nine acts," he said. "The salesperson has to serve as the director to keep the action flowing properly." Pointing to the card, he began to outline the Action Selling system like this:

Act 1: Commitment Objective. This act takes place before the sales call begins. Prior to calling on any customer, the salesperson must set a Commitment Objective — that is, a goal specifying an action the salesperson wants the customer to agree to take. The salesperson might have other objectives, such as to conduct an analysis of the customer's needs, but a Commitment Objective is special in that it requires the customer to agree to *do* something that will move the sales process forward: agree to schedule a meeting with other decision makers, agree to grant preferred-vendor status to the salesperson's company, agree to buy the product, or something similar.

"Calling on a customer without a specific Commitment Objective in mind is unprofessional."

Action Selling says that calling on a customer without a specific

Commitment Objective in mind is unprofessional. It wastes the time of both the customer and the salesperson, because if a call doesn't move the sales process forward in some way, what's the point?

"No Commitment Objective, no call," Scott said, stating a cardinal rule of Action Selling.

> *"No Commitment Objective, no call."*

"But this applies only to calls on prospects, not to calls on existing customers?" Christine asked.

"Oh, no, it applies to any call," Scott said. "I'm sure I had a Commitment Objective for my call on Dr. Wright. But then Susan sandbagged me with the disinfectant thing, and I...."

"Never mind," Christine said. "Please go on."

So Scott continued to describe the Action Selling process.

Act 2: People Skills. Since the customer's first major buying decision is whether to buy the sales rep, the rep's first task is to sell himself. ("Or herself, of course," Scott added.) In fact, the decision about whether to buy the salesperson is so important that Action Selling devotes three acts to it. In the first of these, the salesperson calls upon his interpersonal skills to demonstrate that he is likeable, friendly, and trustworthy. The salesperson must show that he is genuinely interested in the customer as a person. The salesperson does this mainly by demonstrating excellent listening skills. He *asks* the customer open-ended questions to get to know the customer and the customer's company. Then he listens carefully to the answers.

"And once the salesperson has established rapport," Christine said, "what other types of open-ended questions might he ask?"

"Well, I'll tell you," Scott said, smiling because he knew Christine was cueing him to move on to Act 3. He flipped the laminated card to show the "Ask the Best Questions Map" on its reverse side.

Act 3: Ask the Best Questions. Action Selling teaches that most of the "selling" that takes place in a call occurs in Act 3, before the product has even been discussed and with the customer doing most of the talking. By Asking the Best Questions, the salesperson uncovers vital information that will later allow him to present his company and his products in a manner custom-tailored to the customer's particular needs and concerns.

As the map shows, the Best Questions fall into categories. Some have to do with the salesperson's position and what strategy to take for making the sale: Which of the salesperson's competitors is the customer considering? How urgent is the buying decision? Who else in the customer's organization will be involved in the decision? Other categories have questions designed to uncover specific needs that the salesperson believes his company or products could

The most useful needs to uncover are those in which the customer has a personal, emotional stake.

address effectively — needs that hopefully correspond to the strengths of his products or services.

The most useful needs to uncover are those in which the customer has a personal, emotional stake. A problem may belong to the customer's company, but how does he himself win if the company's problem is solved? If more than one person is involved in the buying decision, how does each of them win by solving the problem? In Action Selling, questions designed to uncover those high-yield, personal needs are called Leverage Questions.

"Remind me," said Christine: "What's the point of all this questioning again?"

"For one thing, it helps me 'sell myself' by showing that I care about the customer's real needs," Scott said. "But it also allows me to identify ways to be different and better when the customer makes buying decisions about my company and my product."

"You mean that by Asking the Best Questions the salesperson learns how he could add value by selling something more than the price of a generic bottle of disinfectant?" Christine asked.

Scott shifted uncomfortably in his chair. "Well, yeah, but..."

"Sorry again for interrupting," Christine said. "You're doing great. Please continue."

Act 4: Agree on Need. When the salesperson feels he has

uncovered at least three high-yield needs that his products or services could address effectively, he confirms his understanding with the customer. "As I understand it," the salesperson says, "you're looking for something that will do X, Y, and Z. Is that correct?"

This accomplishes three things. First, it demonstrates again that the salesperson cares about the customer's needs and has listened carefully to the description of them. Trust is built while the salesperson demonstrates sincere interest in the customer. Second, it cements and clarifies those needs in the customer's own mind. Third, it sets the agenda for the rest of the call because the salesperson now can gear his presentation to problems and opportunities that the customer already has agreed are important.

"That sounds like a critical step," said Christine.

Act 4:
- *Shows you care*
- *Cements the needs*
- *Sets the call agenda*

"It's huge. And it's one of the things I didn't do before I learned about Action Selling," Scott admitted.

Act 5: Sell the Company. Up to this point, the salesperson has been "selling himself" — and doing so, ironically, by letting the customer do most of the talking. Now the salesperson takes center stage to address the customer's second major buying decision by describing his company and its capabilities. Instead of launching into a canned presentation, however, the salesperson is now able to customize his description of the company in succinct terms that correspond to the specific needs the customer has already agreed upon. What can the salesperson's company do to solve this customer's problems that its competitors are unable or unlikely to do just as well?

You understand Action Selling just fine, Scott, Christine was starting to think. *Your problem is that you aren't applying what you know to situations with your current accounts. We might be able to fix this.*

Act 6: Sell the Product. Still focusing on the needs agreed upon in Act 4, the salesperson presents his products or services in a way that demonstrates how they would address the needs of this particular customer. Instead of the classic "data dump" presentation including many product details that may be irrelevant to the customer, the salesperson targets the product presentation.

> *Instead of a "data dump," you target the product presentation.*

"So you tie everything you present back to a need you agreed upon in Act 4, right?" Christine pointed to the appropriate spot on the colorful card.

"That's right," Scott said. "Now, this next act is my favorite."

Act 7: Ask for Commitment. In Act 1, the salesperson established a Commitment Objective, a plan for an action to which the customer should agree. If the salesperson wants the customer's commitment, however, he must ask for it. ("I was stunned in the

Action Selling training program when I realized how often I'd been failing to do that," Scott added.) If the commitment he wants is a buying decision, the salesperson quickly summarizes the product features that appealed to the customer, quotes the price and asks, "How does that sound?" If the customer agrees that it sounds good, the salesperson says, "Would you like to go ahead with it?"

"If I run into stalls or objections, Action Selling has great ways

"I realized how often I'd been failing to Ask for Commitment."

to deal with them," Scott said. "Want to hear about those?"

"Not right now," Christine said. "Please go ahead."

Act 8: Confirm the Sale. After the customer has agreed to buy, the salesperson insures against buyer's remorse by doing three things: *Assure* the customer that he has made the right decision. Thank the customer and tell him that you *appreciate* the business. And schedule a *future event* that the customer can anticipate to take his mind off the money he just spent.

"Okay, that's the sales call," Scott said. "After the call, we analyze what happened."

Act 9: Replay the Call. According to Action Selling, every time true professional salespeople complete a call they conduct a mental review of the drama to determine what they did well and what they could have done better. Were there additional questions they should have asked in Act 3? Could their product presentation in Act 6 have been more succinct and better targeted to the customer's agreed-upon needs? Pros replay every call, looking for ways to improve their performance. They never stop honing their skills.

"That's it," Scott said, "the Reader's Digest version of Action Selling."

"Well, you certainly seem to understand the system," Christine said. "And you say you've found it helpful in calls on new clients?"

Every time true professional salespeople complete a call they conduct a mental review.

"'*Helpful*' doesn't begin to describe it," Scott said. "It's fantastic. I never felt so confident or so much in control of my sales calls as I do now."

"But you don't quite see how Action Selling can help you fight price competition and protect your margins when you call on your established customers. For example, when a dentist's office manager finds a cheaper price on disinfectant, you don't know what to do except match the price. And you think you need something other than the Action Selling system — a training course in negotiation skills — to help you with that problem. Do I have that right?" Christine asked.

"I have a feeling you think I've been missing something," Scott said.

"Let's see if we can figure out what it might be," Christine replied. "I have a feeling that you're going to kick yourself pretty soon. But I also have a feeling that you're going to leave this office a lot happier than you were when you walked in."

Chapter 2

YOU'RE NEVER OUTSIDE THE SYSTEM

The commodity trap, and how to avoid it.

C hristine rose and walked to her desk. She grabbed a document from the cluttered desktop and returned to the conference table.

"Scott, you mentioned that a salesperson can develop relationships with customers that the Internet and direct mail can't match," she said. "Here's some research that agrees with you. This is a white paper from The Sales Board, the company that created the Action Selling system. It reports the results of a nationwide study of salespeople and sales executives about the very problem you've got: price competition."

She turned to a page of summary findings. "Sales executives say that the Number 1 reason customers buy from their company instead of the competition is due to the customer's relationship with a salesperson."

That sounded encouraging. Scott leaned forward attentively.

"But there's a little more to it," Christine warned. "Eighty-six percent of sales executives agree that top salespeople generate higher margins than average ones." She looked him in the eye. "That suggests to me that top salespeople must handle price conversations differently than average ones. Wouldn't you agree?"

No longer encouraged, Scott just nodded.

"Here are two more findings about the difference between top sales reps and average ones," she said. "Eight out of 10 sales executives say that *most* of their salespeople are ineffective at dealing with price objections. And they say that the No. 1 reason why average sales reps fail to get their price is because they fail to differentiate themselves from the competition.

"It seems to me," Christine continued, "another way to say that is that an average sales rep's customers see his products as undistinguishable. Which means that the only difference customers are likely to see between his products and the competition's is the price. Which means there actually isn't a whole lot of difference between that average salesperson and a direct-mail flyer."

Scott's self-image as a talented, veteran sales rep was taking a beating. One word kept ringing in his ears. Average. *No, not even average,* he thought. *It's my territory that's dragging the average down.*

> ## Research* says...
>
> *No. 1 reason customers buy from one company instead of another: relationship with the salesperson.*
>
> *Top salespeople generate higher margins than average ones.*
>
> *Most salespeople are ineffective at handling price objections.*
>
> *No. 1 reason for discounting: failure to differentiate.*
>
> * Study of 722 Sales Professionals, Sales Managers, and C-level Executives by The Sales Board, 2004.
> More information at www.thesalesboard.com

He straightened his shoulders. "Christine, you don't have to convince me I'm doing something wrong," he said. "The fact that our other reps are getting better margins — and that I'm working harder for less money — is all the evidence I need."

Christine liked his answer. *He's ready to make a change. And maybe there's an opportunity here,* she thought, her mind racing ahead to the call she expected from her regional manager. *If I can straighten out Scott, I'll be on top of my branch's margin problem when Gary calls about it. And if Scott can do it, why not all of our Scotts, nationwide?* She began to picture her conversation with the regional manager in a new light: *"Gary, I've got something I think you and I should take to corporate..."* She realized that Scott had begun talking again.

"The problem is," he said, "we're mainly a reseller. Most of the things I sell to dentists on a regular basis *are* commodities:

disinfectant, cotton rolls, latex gloves, X-ray film..."

"Deciding whether to buy is always the sum of a combination of factors."

"All right, stop," Christine said sharply. "Here's the first change we're going to make: I don't want to hear the word 'commodity' again in connection with Partner Dental. Scott, *nothing* you sell is a plain commodity. Every time customers choose to buy from you — or not to — they aren't choosing in a vacuum that contains nothing but your product. The thing they're deciding whether to buy is always the sum of a combination of factors: your product, your company, and their personal relationship with you. For better or worse, that combination of factors is always unique. It is never a plain commodity.

"You just told me about the five major buying decisions every customer makes," Christine continued, "the ones that form the basis of Action Selling: salesperson, company, product, price, time-to-buy. How can you turn around now and tell me that you're selling undifferentiated commodities?"

"Okay, I get what you mean," Scott said. "But it's one thing to use Action Selling when I go after a new prospect. I guess I don't see how it works as well when I'm making my regular route calls."

"What's the big difference?" Christine asked.

"Well, with a prospect I can take more time, and I can present myself and Partner Dental as a new opportunity. I can do a more thorough needs analysis. I ask to see the invoices from suppliers they're currently using, and I work up a presentation that shows us as a comprehensive solution to their specific needs. I signed up three of my new clients for our Partner Plus program," he added, referring to Partner Dental's program for regular, high-volume buyers.

"Partner Plus protects our margins while streamlining the dentist's inventory and ordering procedures, right?" Christine said.

"Right. I love Partner Plus."

"What about your other five new clients?" she asked.

Scott's gaze shifted to her office window. "Well, Partner Plus wouldn't have worked for them."

"You got that business by beating the competition's prices, didn't you," Christine said. It wasn't a question.

"Well it was more than…," he began. *Oh, what the heck.* "Yeah, essentially that's what I did," he admitted.

"So you say the competition is murdering *you* on price, but in fact you're right in there leading the race to the bargain basement."

> *"You're right in there leading the race to the bargain basement."*

I'm not a salesman, I'm a skunk, Scott thought, miserably. *I stink. Just shoot me now.*

"Let's talk about your regular route customers," Christine said. "What do you usually do when someone like Susan the office manager tells you she's found a lower price on something like disinfectant or cotton rolls?"

"Usually I match the price," Scott said, no longer attempting to disguise his failures.

"What happens when you don't match the competitor's price?"

He smiled bitterly. "Last month I told a dental assistant that I couldn't match a price on latex gloves. I went back the next week, and there in the storage room was a year's supply of latex gloves from SaveMore Dental. That's about par for the course."

> *"You're actually teaching them to object to your price."*

Christine felt a pang of sympathy. "And episodes like that have taught you that if a dentist wants a discount, you'd better give him one?"

Scott just nodded.

"But that becomes a vicious circle, doesn't it?" Christine asked. "Pretty soon your customers figure out that if they want a lower price from you — and they always do — all they have to do is ask. In fact, they'd be fools *not* to ask. You're actually teaching them to object to your price. When Susan waved that flyer from Discount Dental at you, she was only doing exactly what you've encouraged her to do, wasn't she?"

Scott had never looked at it that way. "I guess you're right," he said, thoughtfully. "It's as if I'm helping to create a system of discounting — a culture where price-haggling is normal. I took a vacation last year, and it really struck me how different the whole concept of shopping is when you go to a resort or deal with a beach vendor. Nothing has a set price. You're expected to haggle. The vendors think you're an ignorant jerk if you *don't* haggle with them. Geez, have I managed to turn myself into one of those guys who sells straw hats to tourists?"

> *"You gave away almost $50,000 in profits last year, a buck at a time."*

Christine laughed. *There's a line for my national training program,* she thought. "So you agree that when you fall into the discounting habit, you only encourage your clients to ask for more discounts?" she asked.

"Yes," Scott said.

"And thanks to that discounting habit, you gave away almost $50,000 in profits last year, a buck at a time?"

This just keeps getting worse, he thought. *Help!* "Yes," he said aloud. "How do I break the habit?"

"It seems to me you already know," Christine said. "When you wcre explaining the nine acts of Action Selling, you said that in Act 7 you Ask for Commitment. And you said that if you hear an objection instead, Action Selling offers you a great way to deal with it."

"Sure," Scott protested. "But that's when I'm working inside the Action Selling system. I've built momentum, I've made a presentation, I've asked for commitment, and I hear a price objection. That's different from when I walk in the door on a route call and Susan shows me a flyer with a cheaper price on the same commod... on the same product I sell."

Christine's head was shaking before he finished. "Scott, with Action Selling you're *always* inside the system. There's no such thing as 'outside the system.' What you got from Susan was an objection — a price objection. What does Action Selling tell you to do when you hear an objection?"

"With Action Selling you're always inside the system."

Scott sighed. "I go back to Act 3," he said.

"In Act 3 you Ask the Best Questions, right? How does that help you?"

"When I hear an objection, I'm supposed to ask questions that let me do three things: understand the objection, quantify it, and identify options. But Christine, I already understand Susan's objection. She has been ordered to cut costs, and somebody else is offering her a lower price on the same disinfectant I sell."

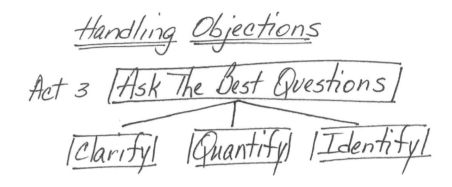

"Scott, didn't you say that listening is a critical skill in Acts 2 and 3?" Christine asked. "When did Action Selling ever tell you that you can *stop* listening to customers whenever you aren't in the middle of a formal needs analysis?"

"Huh?"

"You heard Susan say, 'I can get a lower price on this disinfectant.' But you didn't really hear the part where she said, 'I've been ordered to cut costs on consumables.' Doesn't that sound like the kind of customer need you'd be looking to uncover if you *were* in the middle of Act 3? Isn't the whole point of Asking the Best Questions to discover needs like the one Susan just handed you on a silver platter?"

That's when the light bulb clicked on in Scott's head. Christine saw the realization hit him. *That's right, Buddy,* she thought. *You know how to do this. You just haven't been applying it to everyday selling situations.*

"Sometimes you don't take the customer to Act 3," she said softly, as if reading his mind. "Sometimes the customer takes you."

> ## *"Sometimes you don't take the customer to Act 3. Sometimes the customer takes you."*

For several seconds Scott looked vacant, as lost opportunities ran through his mind. Finally he spoke again. "You said I was going to kick myself." He made a "clunk" sound with his tongue. "Did you ever see one of those old Looney Tunes cartoons where Yosemite Sam or somebody has a big boot on a stick with a rope attached, and when he's done something stupid he yanks on the rope to kick himself in the butt? I wish I had that contraption right now."

Another line for my national training program, Christine thought. *Thanks, Scott.*

She grinned at him. "I also said that you were going to come out of this a happier guy. Now, when Susan objects to our price on a particular item like disinfectant, and she happens to mention that she has been ordered to cut costs on consumables, how do you think we ought to respond?"

Scott's dejection lifted as his thoughts turned from the lost past to a far more promising future. "We go straight to Act 3, and we start asking questions to let us understand Susan's objection, quantify it, and look for options," he said excitedly. "Why has Dr. Wright told you to cut costs? What specific target did he give you, like a percentage of overall consumable costs you're supposed to cut? Which products are a special concern? Let's see…"

Christine joined in. "Who else are you currently buying from? How much are you buying from each supplier? Who else in the office is supposed to be helping to cut consumable costs?"

> *"With an Objection, we go straight to Act 3, and ask questions."*

Scott grabbed the thread again. "How will Dr. Wright know if you're successful? Will you give him some kind of report?"

"And I believe you said something earlier about 'leverage questions,'" Christine said. "Aren't those supposed to get at the customer's personal, emotion stake in the issue?"

"Right you are," Scott said, happily. "How does Susan herself win if she is successful at solving this problem? The problem she and I are now working on together, as partners, because I finally had sense enough to ASK HER A QUESTION!"

Christine leaned over the table to give Scott a high five. "*Now* you sound like an Action Selling pro," she said.

Chapter 3

A SOLUTION TO WHAT?

Differentiate or die — a buck at a time.

cott and Christine walked up the hallway to grab some coffee from the pot near the receptionist's desk. When they returned to Christine's office, he said, "Do you have time to walk me through my next call on Dr. Wright? I'd like to tell you I understand Action Selling well enough to know exactly what to do now that you've pried my eyes open, but we've already established that I need to make some changes."

Christine smiled. "You mean that instead of a route, you've been in a rut. And now you want to change that, beginning with Dr. Wright?" *You've been acting like an order-taker, not a salesperson,* she thought.

"A rut instead of a route. Yeah, that's exactly what I've been in," Scott said. "I've been making my route calls without a real plan. Instead of acting, I've just been reacting. But no more."

"OK," Christine said. "Let's start with your overall goal. What is it that you want to accomplish with customers like those at Dr. Wright's office?"

Scott thought about the question for a while. "I want to do what

> *"Action Selling told me to be a consultant with a purpose."*

Action Selling told me I should *always* do," he finally said. "I want to be a consultant with a purpose. When I walk into a customer's office, I don't want them to say, 'Oh, here's Scott. How are we fixed for cotton rolls and how much is he charging?' I want them to be excited to see me."

"You want them to be excited because you've become a valuable contributor to their business strategy?" Christine asked.

"Right. I need to differentiate myself, and I don't want the differentiating factor to be price. I want to offer a solution that adds value in the customer's eyes — something that gives the client a reason to buy from me even though I might charge more for something like a bottle of disinfectant. I want to take the focus *off* which supplier is offering the lowest price this month. I want the competition's next flyer to be irrelevant."

"It sounds like you don't just want to sell more to Dr. Wright, you want to sell more at a higher margin," Christine said.

"Yes, that too. I'd like to be able to differentiate from the competition even if our basic products appear to be the same."

"Good," Christine said. "And how can you use Action Selling to achieve those goals?"

Again Scott took a moment to think. "It starts with Commitment Objectives," he said. "I think I've been making a mistake by seeing them only as commitments I want from the customer for my own reasons. If

> *Commitment Objectives don't just move me closer to a sale; they move the customer closer to a solution.*

I'm really selling solutions and not commodities, the Commitment Objectives I set for every call don't just move me closer to a sale; they move the customer closer to a solution for an important business need. If I go into every sales call with a Commitment Objective tied to the customer's needs and not just to my desire to make a sale, then it isn't only the sales process that's moving forward every time I show up. It's the customer's business strategy that's moving forward."

"That's exactly right, Scott," Christine said. "And you become a key player in that strategy. Pretty soon you won't have to compete with every discount flyer that comes into a dentist's office — or even with our competitors' territory reps. You'll be far more valuable to your clients."

"Starting with a Commitment Objective, that's really what the whole Action Selling process enables me to do, isn't it?" he said.

"And the salesperson who manages the sales process the best is the one who wins."

> *"The salesperson who manages the sales process the best is the one who wins."*

You really are starting to get it now, Christine thought. "Another way to say that," she said, "might be that if you want 'customer loyalty' from Dr. Wright and his staff, you won't get it just by showing up on your route calls and being a nice guy. You'll have to earn it somehow. Do I have that right?"

"Exactly."

"And you said you intend to start earning that loyalty by exploring their needs," Christine said. "But to be in a position to earn the loyalty you want, you have to uncover needs that you can do something about.   What does Action Selling suggest that you do to identify needs for the special features of your products or your company's services?"

"Oh, yeah," Scott said. "Action Selling calls it Back-Tracking Benefits. I think Dr. Wright is a candidate for our frequent buyer program, Partner Plus. Like a lot of our customers, he buys products from three or four suppliers. We're one of them. If I can sign him up for Partner Plus, I could get more of his business, *and* protect my margins, *and* probably save him some substantial money when all of their costs for acquisition are considered. At the very least I could simplify his ordering and inventory process, which would save time and money. That's the solution I have in mind."

"So to Back-Track Benefits, you'll ask questions designed to uncover needs for which Partner Plus would be a good solution?" Christine wrote some quick notes on a sheet of paper:

Back-Track Benefits

1. Analyze Your Selling Strengths
2. Predict the Needs Satisfied by These Strengths
3. Develop Open-Ended Questions to Draw Out these Needs

"I remember how that works," Scott said.

"All right, let's go with that," Christine said. "But let's also remember that programs like Partner Plus aren't the only option we've got to differentiate ourselves in customers' eyes."

"Right."

Do you really know that? Christine thought. *I wonder. But first things first.*

"So, who are the people in Dr. Wright's business whom you'll have to sell on Partner Plus?" Christine asked. "Could Susan the office manager sign up for the program on her own initiative?"

Scott frowned. "I doubt it," he said. "In fact, I'm sure Dr. Wright would have to OK the decision. He also has a dental assistant and two hygienists who get involved in ordering products. They tell Susan what they need, and sometimes they do the ordering themselves."

"Sounds as if you've got a classic sales situation, with three different kinds of buyers in the picture, all of whom must be sold," Christine said.

"A lot of salespeople think that if they can just reach the UDM, their problems are over."

Seeing Scott's blank look, she elaborated. "In every business-to-business selling situation, you have a single *ultimate decision maker* or UDM — Dr. Wright in this case. That's the person with the authority to make the final buying decision. A lot of salespeople think that if they can just reach the UDM, their problems are over — they don't have to bother selling anybody else.

"Big mistake," Christine continued. "Because the UDM usually will rely on input from two other types of buyers. First, there are *user buyers* — the people who actually use the product or who manage the users. For most of our products, your users are the dental assistant and the hygienists.

"Second, there is what's ordinarily called *specialist buyers*. In the computer industry, for instance, specialist buyers are the IT staff. The ultimate decision maker might be a CIO, the person who controls the budget, but the CIO isn't going to buy anything without consulting the IT staff and the users."

Scott nodded.

"In your case," Christine said, "Susan is standing in for the specialist buyer. She basically functions as the purchasing manager, right? She keeps track of inventory, orders, billing, and so on?"

3 Types of Buyers

	Specialist	User	UDM
Role:	Screens Options	Uses or Supervises Users	Bottom Line Responsibility
Criteria:	Meets Specifications	Product Performance	Financial Outcome
Goals:		Career Enhancement Job Satisfaction	ROI Efficiency
Commitment:		Recommend	Final Approval

"Right," Scott said. "But wait a minute. If Dr. Wright is the UDM, he's the one I really have to convince, isn't he? He's the only one who can agree to try Partner Plus."

"He's the only one who can say *yes*," Christine corrected. "What's important to remember, though, is that the other two buyer types can always say *no*. They can't make the sale for you, but they can sure kill it: 'Dr. Wright, this so-called solution of Scott's is

"A good plan begins with a Commitment Objective."

going to interfere with our ability to serve patients by doing X, Y, and Z.' No, you need the users and specialist buyers on your side. You want them to be telling Dr. Wright how your solution will help the business, not hurt it. When you said that you and Susan are going to be partners in solving her consumables problem, that was an important insight. Don't lose track of it."

"Gotcha," Scott said. "So I need a plan to sell Partner Plus to all three types of buyers. And as we Action Selling professionals know, a good plan begins with a Commitment Objective."

"And where do Commitment Objectives come from?" Christine asked. "How do we decide what our Commitment Objective for a call ought to be?"

"Commitment Objectives correspond to the milestones in my sales cycle," Scott answered. "Milestones are the important steps that have to be completed leading up to the final sale. In this case…well, let's see, with three types of buyers…"

"Keep it simple," Christine said. "Your milestones will be similar with each kind of buyer. You want to question them all about their needs, with an eye toward looking for ways that Partner Plus could help them, right? And you're hoping to enlist Susan as an ally in this project, so you might have some special milestones involving her."

With a little help from Christine, Scott created a list of sell-cycle milestones.

| Sell Cycle Milestones |

Specialist — Analyze Purchases And Processes → Preview Proposal

User — Product Needs Analysis → Demo Products

UDM — Clarify Financial Performance Goals

(Present Proposal)

Scott circled the "Proposal Meeting" at the bottom of the list. "All three buyer types are at the same proposal meeting," he said.

"The other milestones are likely meetings with the individual buyer types."

"I see you added 'preview proposal' in the Specialist Buyer column and 'demo products' under User Buyer," Christine said when Scott finished his list. "What are those about?"

"Since Susan is going to be my ally, I want to run my proposal past her and get her suggestions before I present it to the whole group," Scott said. "As for 'demo products,' it just occurred to me that I could increase my margins further if I can persuade the dental assistant and the hygienists to try some of our own Partner-brand stuff instead of the major brands they buy now. I've mentioned our house-brand products before and got the brush off. But I'll bet if I can bring up the Partner brand in a conversation about their overall use of consumables, they'll be more receptive."

> *"The Commitment Objective at each milestone is for the customer to agree to proceed to the next milestone."*

"Good ideas," Christine said. *You're not bad, Scott, once you've gotten a shove in the right direction.* "Now, if I understand correctly, your Commitment Objective at each milestone is for the customer to agree to proceed to the next milestone?"

"Right," he said. "For instance, in my initial contact with Susan, the Commitment Objective is that she should agree to the needs analysis. After my needs analysis with Dr. Wright, the Commitment Objective is to get him to agree to the proposal meeting at a specific time. And so on."

"I see. And most of the 'selling' you do with each of these buyers is going to take place when?" Christine asked.

> *"In Act 3, I do most of the selling by listening, not talking."*

"In the needs analysis, which is essentially Act 3 of Action Selling," Scott replied, smiling. "I'll do most of the selling by listening, not talking. If I Ask the Best Questions, I should be able to uncover needs that Partner Plus can fill. Then, at the final proposal meeting, I'll tie my presentation back to those specific needs. I'll explain how Partner Plus would be a good solution for Dr. Wright *and* for Susan *and* for the user-buyers."

> *"The most useful needs are the ones in which the buyer has a personal, emotional stake."*

"That brings us back to what you said earlier about high-yield needs, doesn't it?" Christine asked. "If the most useful needs you can uncover are the ones in which the buyer has a personal, emotional stake, how do you get at those through your questioning?"

Scott hesitated. "Hey, I'm the guy with a rut instead of a route, remember?"

Christine laughed. "You're starting with a theory that Partner

Plus is going to be your solution, right? It helps if you also start with some theories about what your customers' high-yield needs might look like. For instance, I'd guess that Dr. Wright wants the best possible ROI on his investment in consumables. I'll bet that's a high-priority issue for him far more than it is for the other types of buyers — because it's *his* money that is buying the consumables."

"Yeah, good," Scott said, making a note. "What else?"

"Nah-uh," Christine said. "Let's think about this together."

They worked up a short list of categories into which the high-yield needs of each buyer type were likely to fall. They divided them into Needs for the Features of their solution and Needs for the Benefits that those features will provide.

High-Yield Needs		
	Specialist	User	UDM
Needs for Features >	Meets Specs.	Product Performance	Financial Outcome
Needs for Benefits >	Career Enhancement	ROI	
	Job Satisfaction		Efficiency

"So in Action Selling terms," Christine said, "you want to surface needs for the most impactful features and benefits of Partner Plus with Act 3 questions. Then you want the various buyers to agree on them in Act 4. Is that right?"

"Yes."

"Well then, what kinds of questions might you use to bring those needs to the surface?"

"Based on the list, I'd need a slightly different set of questions for each buyer type," Scott said. "I'll want each buyer to discuss their high-yield needs candidly, so when I present Partner Plus I can tie the personal needs to my solution. If I can do that, I'm sure they'll quit concentrating on the price of individual items."

Christine studied him. "You know what?" she said. "It feels to me like a professional sales call is about to happen."

Chapter 4

SELL THE RIGHT VALUE TO THE RIGHT PEOPLE

It's not what you sell, it's how.

Christine leaned back in her chair and gazed out the office window, collecting her thoughts.

"Let me see if I understand your strategy," she said. "You have identified a customer need, which is to cut consumable costs. The customer is now trying to do that by viewing products as commodities and shopping for the lowest price on each individual item. This forces you to discount those items, which undercuts your margins and leads to a vicious circle of more discounting. You think that this kind of price shopping is self-defeating for the customer, too, because it's an inefficient way to manage costs. So you want to go back to Dr. Wright's office and propose some meetings with Susan and the other buyers to discuss a long-term solution for managing overall acquisition costs. Am I right so far?"

"Right," Scott said.

"OK. Now, you think the answer to both of these problems — the customer's product-cost issue and your margin issue — lies in our frequent-buyer program, Partner Plus. If you can uncover needs that Partner Plus would address, you figure you could differentiate yourself from your competitors. Dr. Wright and his staff would stop seeing you as a commodity peddler and begin to view you as a consultant with a purpose, the purpose being to contribute to their business strategy. Still right?"

"Absolutely."

"Well then, I see one little flaw in that reasoning," Christine said. *Time to rock your world again, Scott.* "At the risk of violating my own rule about the word 'commodity,' it seems to me that our Partner Plus program is just as much a commodity as a bottle of surface disinfectant."

Scott was stunned. *What did she just say? I can't have heard that right.* Finally he settled for: "I don't understand."

"Don't most of our major competitors have frequent-buyer programs?" Christine asked. "And don't they all operate pretty much the same way as Partner Plus? Aren't their sales reps going to be talking to Dr. Wright about those programs — if they haven't already? Won't those reps try to explain how their programs can cut total acquisition costs because of features very similar to the ones

Partner Plus offers: consolidated product shipments, better inventory control, and so on?"

Scott felt as if he'd been run over by a truck. "I don't know what to say," he confessed. "I thought I'd seen the light. This is just another tunnel."

"No, but it is just another *product*," Christine replied. "Scott, you're almost there. You almost get it. But what I want you to understand is that the product *really doesn't matter*. Is it something simple, like dental floss or surface

> *"The product really doesn't matter. It isn't what you sell — it's how you sell."*

disinfectant? Something more complicated, like a new way to organize and run a company's purchasing process? It doesn't make much difference, because whatever the product or service is, chances are your competitors can offer something awfully similar, if not identical. Heck, if we do come up with a unique feature, they'll copy it in a week.

"Honestly, truly, and for real, Scott, it isn't *what* you sell that counts — it's *how* you sell," she continued, blazing with conviction as if she wanted to open his skull and force the words inside. "Every competitor you've got wants to find a need for his product and then sell to that need. What counts is the *process* of walking arm in arm with a customer, step by step toward the best solution to their problem. In the end, that's the only thing that counts. Why do you think

Action Selling devotes three Acts to salespeople selling themselves? The salesperson who does that best is the one who wins, period. The execution of that process is what differentiates top salespeople from the rest. It's the only reason anybody will ever see you as a consultant with a purpose and not as some guy who sells commodities."

Scott took a while to digest this. Finally he smiled. "Partner Plus isn't a commodity, and neither is surface disinfectant," he told her. "Because there's no such thing as a commodity."

"You bet your butt there's not," she replied, smiling back. *Ta-da! I think he's got it.*

Back-Tracking Benefits
- *Selling Strengths*
- *Predict Needs*
- *Ask Questions*

"Now, getting back to Doc Wright," Christine said, "I believe we established that you have three types of buyers at his office — a specialist, some users, and an ultimate decision maker. You think you have a total acquisition solution to their overall consumable-cost problem — something that would suit their needs better than item-by-item price shopping. You want to walk arm in arm with them in a discovery process to investigate those needs and see if you're right. You said that Action Selling recommends a process called Back-Tracking Benefits?"

"Right," Scott said. "Starting with my selling strengths — the best features of my product — I predict needs that would be satisfied by those strengths, then ask questions to draw out the needs."

"We talked about the kinds of benefits the different buyer types are likely to care about," Christine said. "Suppose we tie those together with the features of Partner Plus and see what we come up with."

What they came up with was this outline:

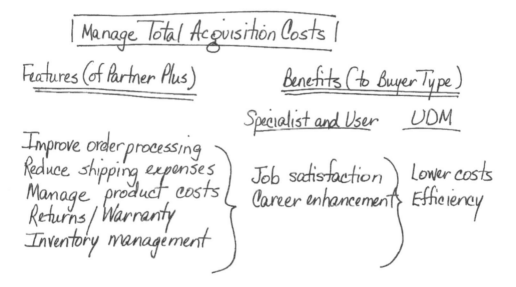

"All right," Christine said, "now you have a map that shows generally where you're trying to go. What does Action Selling recommend as the next step?"

"I need some good questions to ask each buyer type when I meet with them individually to analyze their needs," Scott said. "I want to ask questions that let me *and* the buyers understand exactly how something like improved order processing might increase job satisfaction for the specialist buyer — Susan — and the user buyers. And maybe Dr. Wright cares more about inventory management than he does about a feature like order processing. I need to know that so I'll understand what to stress in my final proposal."

"Do you suppose you and I can come up with all the questions you'll need to ask right now?" Christine asked innocently.

"Oh, no you don't," Scott grinned. "Naturally, new questions will occur to me as I talk to these people because I'll be *listening,*" (He looked at Christine sheepishly.) "But I need a starting point, as well as some questions I want to be sure to ask."

"Back to the drawing board?"

"Yeah, let's do that," Scott said.

They produced a list of questions for each of the three buyer types. The lists looked like this:

Questions for |Specialist Buyer|

  Analyze purchases and processes

Needs for Features:
1. Who do you currently buy from?
2. How do you decide which supplier to buy from?
3. Considering the entire process, what problems can arise from the time you order products until they're in the hands of the people who use them?

Needs for Benefits:
1. When these problems occur, whom do they impact?
2. What effect does that have on your ability to perform your job?

Questions for |<u>User Buyers</u>|

<u>Product</u> <u>Needs</u> <u>Analysis</u>

Needs for Features:

1. What process do you use to decide which products best meet your needs?

2. How do your suppliers help you make those decisions?

3. What problems occur when products don't perform the way you expect them to?

Needs for Benefits:

1. When these problems occur, whom do they impact?

2. What effect does that have on your ability to perform your job?

Questions for [UDM]

Clarify Financial / Performance Goals

Needs for Features:

1. What goals have you set for managing acquisition costs?

2. Other than the price of each individual product, what factors impact your total cost for purchasing and inventory?

Needs for Benefits:

1. With regard to purchasing and inventory management, what problems occur that create inefficiency or added cost?

2. How do you currently measure ROI in these areas?

"These seem like pretty good questions," Christine said when they were finished. "Now what are you going to do with them?"

"I'm calling on Dr. Wright's office again this Thursday," Scott said. "I'll tell Susan I've been thinking about her problem with product costs, and I may be able to help. I'll ask for 15 minutes of her time to discuss it. Those 'specialist' questions are my outline for Act 3 of Action Selling. If I execute the conversation well, she and I should get to Act 4, where we agree on some important needs. She'll begin to see the potential advantages of looking at acquisition costs from a broader perspective. I think she'll agree to help me schedule the meetings with Dr. Wright and the user buyers. She'll be working with me on this as an ally."

"So your meetings with Dr. Wright and the user buyers will probably happen in another call," Christine said. "And you'll agree on needs with them, too?"

> *"I'll be 'selling myself' as a consultant with a purpose during my needs-analysis meetings."*

"Right," Scott said. "All of that represents Acts 3 and 4 of Action Selling. I'll be 'selling myself' as a consultant with a purpose during my needs-analysis meetings with each of the three buyer types. The specific needs we agree upon will show me the best way to sell my company and my product during Acts 5 and 6 at the final proposal meeting with all of the buyers. But before I have that meeting I want to preview the proposal with Susan to make doubly sure that it hits the right targets."

"I like that idea a lot," Christine said. She stood up and looked him in the eye. "Well, Scott, I think you're ready to make a professional sales call."

Scott rose too, but made no move to leave. He seemed to be groping for words. Finally he said, "This was all there in the original Action Selling training program, wasn't it. Everything you've told me about how to escape the price trap was right in front of my eyes. But even though I thought Action Selling was a great system, I didn't see it for what it really is. I can't believe I walked in here and told you I needed a course on negotiating skills."

Christine started to wave the apology aside.

"No," Scott said, holding up his hand. "I guess what I want to say is just...thanks."

Christine smiled. "Go be a consultant with a purpose," she said. "Let me know what happens."

Chapter 5

A CONSULTANT WITH A PURPOSE

Customers are caught in the price trap, too.

T wo weeks later, on a sunny Wednesday morning, a grinning Scott appeared in Christine's office doorway.

"Got a minute?" he asked.

"Sure. Come on in." Christine sized him up as he crossed the room and bounced into a seat at her conference table. "You look like you're having a good day," she observed.

"I'm having a great day," he said happily. "I've had a great two weeks."

"This wouldn't have anything to do with Doc Wright, would it?"

Scott leaned back and laced his fingers behind his head. "Funny you should mention him," he said. "As of yesterday afternoon, Dr. Wright is a participating member in our Partner Plus program — and very glad to be one, I might add. I lowered their acquisition costs,

I increased my share of their business, and I didn't cut my prices."

"That's great, Scott," she said, enjoying his triumph. "Congratulations."

"Christine, using Action Selling with a regular route customer

> **"I lowered their acquisition costs, I increased my share of their business, and I didn't cut my prices."**

was amazing," he said. "I've been calling on the people in Doc Wright's office for almost three years. They like me. We always got along fine. But they *never* opened up about their business like this. And they were happy to do it! It was like, 'Oh, you're actually interested in how this place works? And you might be able to do more for us than take orders and match prices? Well, let us tell you.'

"It was almost embarrassing," he added. "They were perfectly willing to look at me as a consultant with a purpose. All I had to do was act like one."

"You mean that all you had to do was to act like a *better* one than

> **"The salesperson who wins is the one who walks arm-in-arm with the customer toward the best solution."**

your competitors," she corrected him.

"Well, evidently I did something right. Remember when you said that the salesperson who wins is the one who walks arm-in-arm with the customer toward the best solution? We practically skipped."

"It wasn't hard to get them to look at the issue of cutting consumable costs from a broader perspective?" Christine asked.

"Heck no!" Scott said. "When we started talking about things like inventory management and simplifying the ordering process, they saw so many ways we could reduce their headaches that lowering costs became almost a side issue. The fact that Partner Plus will cut their total acquisition cost was like icing on the cake."

"Why don't you walk me through what you did," Christine said.

"That's why I'm here. The last Act of Action Selling, Act 9, is to 'Replay the Call' and look for things you could improve upon next time. May I do that with you?"

"Sure," she said. *And good for you to think of it, Scott.* "Let's start with Act 1, your Commitment Objectives. Did they turn out to be appropriate for the situation or did you have to adjust them at some point?"

"They were the right ones," he said. "Susan the office manager agreed to talk to me about the acquisition-cost issue. Just as I hoped, once she had an idea of the kinds of issues and needs I might be able to help solve, she jumped onto my team and helped arrange meetings with Dr. Wright and the user buyers — the hygienists and the dental assistant. After those meetings, it was no problem gaining everyone's commitment to let me present a proposal."

"How about Act 2?" Christine asked.

People Skills: "I remember names because I write these things down."

"'People skills?' I've gotten to know these people fairly well, so establishing rapport on a personal level at the beginning of the meetings was easier than it is with new prospects. Mostly I asked about their families. I remember the names because I always make a point of writing these things down."

"Good idea. So I take it you were able to move quickly into Act 3 in your meetings with each of the buyer types. How did the questions we prepared for Back-Tracking Benefits of Partner Plus allow you to zero in on high-yield needs? What could you have done better?"

"I hit the jackpot with the question to Susan about what problems arise between the time products are ordered and the time they reach the hands of the users," Scott said. "After nearly half an hour I mentioned that I'd only asked for a few minutes of her time and I was afraid I might be imposing on her too much. She waved me off and went right on talking. Inventory management turned out to be a huge issue, so I asked several more questions to clarify that.

"I thought of asking specifically about inventory management in my meetings with Dr. Wright and the users," he continued. "But I decided to stick with the same kind of broad question about problems that arise after ordering, and see if they'd bring it up themselves. Sure enough, Dr. Wright jumped on inventory. To him, the issues were inefficiency and added costs. As for the users, inventory management was their top concern as a job-satisfaction issue. One of the hygienists, Jennifer, said it drives her insane to walk into the supply room and find a year's worth of cotton rolls but just an empty box of the item she's looking for. It was obvious this had been a source of friction for some time, but they didn't know what to do about it except get mad at one another."

"I think it was smart to stick with your broad questions and let the customers be the ones to bring up inventory manage-

UDM wants Efficiency and ROI. User buyers want Job Satisfaction.

ment," Christine said. "Of course, if you're talking to a different customer next week…"

Scott interrupted to finish the thought. "If I'm Back-Tracking Benefits for Partner Plus with different customers next week, and inventory management doesn't appear on their list of problems, I know the first thing I'm going to ask a question about." *Ahead of you that time, wasn't I, Christine,* he thought. *There's a first.*

"OK, on to Act 4," she said. "In your meetings with each of the three buyer types, what agreement did you reach on their needs with respect to a solution for their acquisition-cost problem?"

"By the end of those meetings it was clear we weren't just talking about how to cut product costs. I mean, sure, Dr. Wright looked at things from the standpoint of ROI as well as efficiency. For the others, efficiency was mainly a question of reducing their own headaches. But in the end, everyone agreed they needed a solution that would do three things. One, improve inventory management. Two, simplify the ordering process. Three, reduce the total cost and the inefficiencies associated with product acquisition."

"Let me guess," Christine said: "Susan was the main driver behind the need to simplify the ordering process."

"Right. The users liked that idea too, but Susan loved it. Turns out she was sick of thumbing through brochures and flyers for this

Price Shopping actually makes the buyer feel unprofessional.

week's lowest prices on stuff like disinfectant. And she was sick of haggling with me and other sales reps. She saw the whole game as an annoying waste of time. She said it made her feel unprofessional, as if she were always rummaging through grocery coupons instead of running a professional operation. Christine, *the price-shopping thing was as big a pain for her as it was for me!"*

Scott shook his head in self-reproach. "Like I said, it was kind of embarrassing. Once we got into the consulting process I really expected Susan to call me on it: 'Do you mean that all this time you've had a way out of the price trap for both of us? Why the heck didn't we do this a year ago?' She never said it, but I'm pretty sure she was thinking it."

Yeah, me too, Christine thought. *Or at least, why didn't you do it as soon as you learned about Action Selling?* Again she envisioned a national follow-up program for Partner Dental's sales reps. *Definitely,* she decided.

"I figured that Susan might be an ally," Scott continued, "but I had no idea of the kind of support I'd get. When she helped me fine-tune my proposal before I presented it to the whole group, that proposal was *hers*. She owned it. "

"Well then, never forget the moment when you realized that she had taken ownership," Christine said. "Remember what it looked like and felt like. Because that's how you'll always know when you've been acting like a consultant with a purpose and not like some guy who sells commodities."

She waited for Scott to digest that. Then she said, "Tell me about Acts 5 through 8 in your proposal meeting. How did you manage to sell your company and product solution, ask for commitment, and confirm the sale, all in the course of a single proposal meeting yesterday afternoon?"

Scott's grin returned. "It works just like Action Selling says, doesn't it? When I sell my company and my product simply by explaining how we can provide the best solution to important needs the customers have already agreed to, I don't have to put everyone to sleep with a

Solution:
Tie Features
to the Needs
identified earlier.

60-minute PowerPoint presentation. I just tied back the features of Partner Plus to the key needs we had identified. It wasn't difficult to show how Partner Plus will simplify ordering and straighten out their inventory-control problems; that's what it's designed to do. And the savings they'll get from consolidated shipments alone will reduce their costs as much as any amount of discount shopping they could do."

"So when you asked for commitment at the end of your presentation, you got it?"

"And they were glad to give it," he said.

"What about Act 8 — Confirm the Sale? I'm sure you thanked them and assured them they were making the right decision. What 'future event' did you recommend to ward off buyer's remorse?"

"I set an appointment for Friday afternoon to train Susan and the users on the online-ordering function on the Partner Plus web site," he said. "They won't really need my help much, if at all, but they're looking forward to getting started."

Christine considered everything he had told her. "You obviously did a good job," she said. "Now, if there was one part of the process where you think you could have handled things better, what would it be?"

Scott already had given that some thought. "In yesterday's presentation meeting, I think I went on a little too long about how

Partner Plus could cut total acquisition costs. Sure, that was the original issue, but Dr. Wright was satisfied with the cost piece before I quit talking about it. Even he was really more interested in streamlining the whole acquisition process. He asked a few questions about inventory that I hadn't anticipated. Nothing I couldn't handle — but I think I was slow to appreciate how much the emphasis in the whole deal had shifted away from cutting costs and toward managing the purchasing process."

> *"The whole deal shifted from cutting costs to managing the purchasing process."*

"Let me see if I understand," Christine said. "When we spoke before, you realized that sometimes a customer takes *you* to Act 3, instead of vice versa. Your signal was Susan's statement that Doc Wright had told her to cut costs when she asked you to lower your price on surface disinfectant. In your sales calls at Doc Wright's office over the past two weeks, you learned that a customer's *stated* need isn't necessarily the real need. Sometimes customers don't understand their needs, and your consulting assistance can help them enormously."

"Yep," Scott said. "And before you say it, I need to *listen* to what the customer is telling me and then use my Action Selling skills in every single sales call. I made 50,000 one-dollar mistakes last year. I'm done doing that."

> ## "I made 50,000 one-dollar mistakes last year. I'm done doing that."

Christine regarded him with satisfaction. "Well Scott," she said, "correct me if I'm wrong, but you seem to have concluded that Action Selling applies to regular route customers just as much as to new prospects. You also seem to feel that it offers you a way out of the commodity trap and a way to protect your margins — an alternative to competing on price alone in a race to the bargain basement. Is that correct?"

"Yes," he agreed sheepishly. "I don't know why I didn't get it the first time, but I get it now."

"Then I have just one more question. How interested are you in me finding you a training course on price negotiation?"

Scott was still laughing when he left Christine's office, as if that were the funniest idea he ever heard.

Epilogue

Are you earning your keep?

C hristine placed her notes on the podium and looked out past the stage lights at the sea of faces in the hotel ballroom. Partner Dental sales reps from all over North America gazed back at her expectantly. She adjusted the microphone and took a breath. *Here goes*, she thought.

"Good morning. I'm Christine Cooper, branch manager in Los Angeles. Matt Simon, our CEO, will address you in a moment. But he asked me to kick things off because I'm the one who lobbied him to schedule this training event. If you're looking for the guilty party, I guess I'm it."

The line drew the polite chuckles she expected.

"Last year, in this same venue, we introduced a new sales system called Action Selling. The feedback we've received from all of you says that you have found it enormously valuable. Our North American sales figures say the same thing.

"As you know, Action Selling is a systematic approach to managing and conducting the entire sales process, from initial contact with a prospect to following up after the sale. But Action Selling offers another opportunity that isn't necessarily obvious. Some of you recognized it the first time around. For you, this two-day training event will be a chance to hone and refine skills you're already using.

"Others, however, are in for a major revelation. You're going to be especially happy that you came here today.

"What is the hidden opportunity I'm talking about? It's that Action Selling doesn't just give you a dependable way to close more sales, gain new business, and wind up with more satisfied customers. That you already know. What some of you don't quite get yet is that Action Selling also gives you a way to protect your *margins* in the face of brutal price competition.

"Action Selling isn't just a better way to sell your products. It's a way to *sell your price* — both to new customers and to established ones.

"Like a lot of industries, ours is engaged in what I think of as a race to the bargain basement. A lot of factors play into it. There's the increasing commodification of products and services — including 'value-add' strategies such as our Partner Plus program, which looks a lot like other frequent-buyer programs. There's the consolidation of suppliers into fewer, larger competitors. And let's not forget the

Internet, which makes price shopping much easier. The upshot is that every day we are under intense pressure to match or beat our competitors' lowest prices.

"Tell me if this sounds familiar: You make a call on a regular route customer. The office manager shows you a brochure or a catalog from one of our competitors. They're running a special on some of the items we sell — cotton rolls, surface disinfectant, or whatever. There they are, in black and white: the very same products, a few bucks cheaper.

"Well, what can you do? If you want to keep the business, you figure, you'll have to discount. So you match the competitor's price."

Some uncomfortable shuffling in the audience told Christine that, yes, that sounded familiar to a number of the reps.

"I know a Partner salesperson who gave away $50,000 in profits last year, a buck at a time, by doing exactly that. He thought the solution would be to improve his negotiating skills somehow.

"He doesn't think so anymore. And he isn't discounting to keep his business anymore. Because he figured out that the answer isn't to get better at haggling over price. The answer is to get out of the price-negotiation game altogether. The solution is not to run faster or run smarter in the race to the bargain basement. It's to withdraw from that race altogether and start running a different one.

"The answer, he realized, is Action Selling.

"Why? Because Partner's business strategy is to compete on value, not on price. If you want to compete on value, you must offer the customer a valid reason to pay a little more to deal with you instead of with your competitors. In a world of commodified products, commodified services, and now commodified value-add strategies, you cannot differentiate or add value to your offerings based on *what* you sell. You can only do it based on *how* you sell.

"What my friend realized is that the salesperson who wins is the one who does the best job of executing a *process* in which the salesperson and the customer walk arm-in-arm toward a solution that will best serve the customer's needs. That process is the whole ballgame. Executing it better than the other guys do is the only sustainable way to differentiate ourselves and to add lasting value in the customer's eyes. It's the only thing our competitors can't copy.

"My friend knew, of course, that the Action Selling system puts 'price' in its proper context as only one of five major elements in the customer's buying decision. But he didn't quite get the implications. Now he does.

"He had a few other revelations as well. He realized that every time he caved into pressure to discount his products to match a competitor's offer, he was actually teaching his customers to object to his prices. He was encouraging and rewarding them for focusing on the price of each individual item he sells. He wasn't just a victim in the race to the bargain basement; he was helping to perpetuate it. That was not a pleasant discovery.

"But he also got a very pleasant surprise. He learned that some of his clients — maybe most of them — were as unhappy as he was with the price-shopping game. They saw the endless cycle of bargain hunting as a frustrating waste of time and energy. They were glad to find a reason to justify opting out of it. All my friend really had to do was to give them that justifiable reason.

"Like my friend, I am a salesperson, management title or not. I love this profession. But price competition has brought our profession to a critical juncture. Because if customers see our products and services as commodities, and they make buying decisions based solely or primarily on price, it's hard to see a reason why a company should continue to maintain a professional sales force. There are too many cheaper ways to match or beat competitors' low-price offers. If that's all salespeople do, then they just become extra overhead. They're not earning their keep. If Partner Dental or any other company is running a race to the bargain basement, salespeople's salaries and commissions are nothing but a drag on performance.

"As salespeople, we *must* find ways to add value that gives customers a reason to buy from us on some basis besides price. Otherwise, what are we doing on the payroll?

Christine paused to let that sink in.

"Here's the good news: We know for a fact that *how* you sell is the key factor in winning your price. Top salespeople not only sell more than average ones, they also generate higher margins. We can prove that with breakdowns of our own sales figures. It's also demonstrated by research.

"The Sales Board recently conducted a National Price Competition Study. A white paper describing the complete results is included in the handouts you'll be receiving. But let me cite just two key findings.

"First is the one I just mentioned: Overwhelmingly and across all industries, respondents agree that top salespeople drive higher margins than average ones. That can only mean there is a significant difference not in what they sell, but in how they sell.

"Second, respondents say that the No. 1 reason why customers choose them over their competitors is because of a relationship with a salesperson. That relationship is more important than product characteristics. And it's more important than price.

"To protect our margins and win our price, what kind of relationship do we need to cultivate with our customers? I like the way my friend put it. 'When they see me coming,' he said, 'I don't want them to say, 'Oh, here's what's-his-name. I wonder how much he's charging for cotton rolls this week.' Instead, my friend wants his customers to say, 'Oh, good, here he is. I'll bet he has another idea that will help us run our business.'

"It doesn't matter whether the problem involves inventory or some other business issue. What matters, my friend decided, is that he doesn't want customers to see him as a salesman peddling wares and negotiating prices. He wants them to see him as a consultant with a purpose — the purpose being to help them run their business more effectively. And he knows that the way to get his customers to see him as a consultant with a purpose is to act like one.

"He now knows what some of you have already figured out: Action Selling is not just a sales system. It's actually a blueprint or a set of stage directions that tells you how to act like a consultant with a purpose. And it doesn't apply only in situations where you're starting the sales process from scratch with a new prospect. It applies equally to every regular route customer you've got."

From his seat near the back of the ballroom, Scott sent silent encouragement toward the stage. *You're doing great, Christine*, he thought. *You deserve this moment.* He returned the name she had given to him. *My friend. You won't be my boss much longer, because this company would be crazy not to move you up the ladder. But you might be the best friend I ever had.* He leaned forward in his chair, willing the people around him to listen and learn as Christine wound up her speech.

"We're going to show you how to win your price, protect your margins, and opt out of the race to the bargain basement. Some of you are going to kick yourselves because you didn't see it sooner.

On the management side, we're kicking ourselves because we didn't make it more explicit the first time around.

"Very soon, though, the kicking will stop. You're going to learn that the way to sell your price is not to be a great negotiator but to *stop selling on price*. I mean really stop it, once and for all. The way to win your price is to 'sell yourself.' Action Selling told you that was your first and greatest task, but you don't quite get it yet. You soon will.

"It would be an understatement to say that I think you'll find these next two days eye-opening and productive. Partner Dental is going to make more money — and so are you. I'd wish you good luck, but when you leave here you won't have to depend on luck. So let me just say, Good Action Selling!"

ACTION SELLING
SKILLS ASSESSMENT

TAKE A FREE ASSESSMENT OF YOUR SALES SKILLS!

When you have finished reading this book, go to www.ActionSellingBookAssessment.com for a free assessment of your sales skills.

The 55-question assessment takes approximately 30 minutes to complete. It measures both the knowledge you have gained from the book and your current skill levels in five critical areas of selling: *building a buyer/seller relationship; call planning; questioning skills; presentation skills;* and *gaining commitment.*

In confidential reports like those shown above, your skill scores will be compared to the norms of 200,000 salespeople who have answered the same questions on a more extensive version of the assessment that is part of the Action Selling training program. The reports highlight specific areas in which improving your skills would lead to the biggest boost in sales performance.

ORDER MORE BOOKS!

TO ORDER BOOKS:

- Call (800) 232-3485
- www.ActionSelling.com
- Fax (763) 473-0109
- Mail to The Sales Board

$19.95 Retail
 5.00 Discount
$14.95 Reader Price

QUANTITY	BOOK	BOOK ORDER FORM
☐	Selling Your Price	**SHIPPING AND HANDLING**
☐	Action Selling	$3.95 per US order Can/Int'l actual cost Payable in US funds

THE SALES BOARD
15200 25ᵀᴴ AVE. N.
PLYMOUTH, MN 55447

BILL MY CREDIT CARD

Card# _____ Exp. _____

DISC _____ VISA_____ MC _____ AMEX_____

Signature _____

Bill to _____

Address _____

City _____ ST _____ Zip _____

Daytime phone _____

Ship to _____

Address _____

City _____ ST _____ Zip _____

# of Books _____

Price $ 14.95 _____

Total $_____

MN Sales Tax $_____

Ship/Handling $ 3.95 _____

Total Due $_____

Please allow 5-7 days for US Delivery. Can/Int'l orders pleas allow 10 days.
This offer is subject to change without notice

GET TRAINED AND CERTIFIED AS AN
ACTION SELLING PROFESSIONAL!

Want to learn more about how Action Selling can help your organization realize its full sales potential? For information about training and certification for yourself or your salespeople, contact The Sales Board.

Founded in 1990, The Sales Board has boosted the performance of more than 2,500 companies and 200,000 salespeople worldwide in virtually every industry. Action Selling provides a systematic approach to managing and conducting the entire sales process. Our complete training program provides all the necessary tools for students and instructors. Training is customized specifically for each organization's selling situation and even for individual salespeople.

Studies document that veteran salespeople who become Action Selling Certified improve their sales performance by an annual average of 16 percent. As for rookie salespeople, there is no finer system to start them off on the right foot and make them productive immediately.

Students participate in a highly interactive two-day training session facilitated by our talented trainers or by their own Action Selling Certified managers. Students then take part in Skill Drills to refine and reinforce their new skills in the field. Accountability is built into the process with management reinforcement, plus an assessment and certification system.

To learn more about the complete Action Selling training and certification system, please contact us or visit our Web site:

The Sales Board
(800) 232-3485
info@thesalesboard.com
www.TheSalesBoard.com

ABOUT THE AUTHOR

Duane Sparks is chairman and founder of The Sales Board, a Minneapolis-based company that has trained and certified more than 200,000 salespeople in the system and the skills of Action Selling. He is the author of the Best Selling book, *Action Selling, How to sell like a professional even if you think you are one.*

In a 30-year career as a salesperson and sales manager, Duane has sold products ranging from office equipment to insurance. He was the top salesperson at every company he ever worked for. He developed Action Selling while owner of one of the largest computer marketers in the United States. Even in the roaring computer business of the 1980s, his company grew six times faster than the industry norm, differentiating itself not by the products it offered but by the way it sold them. Duane founded The Sales Board in 1990 to teach the skills of Action Selling to others.